ALEXANDER O. EMOGHENE

HUNGER FOR IMPACT

SOMETHING IS ABOUT TO CHANGE

Hunger For Impact

CONTENTS PAGE

INTRODUCTION

The desire to live a life of impact is not the whimsical idea of the minority; it is a dream for all. People often settle for the ordinary in life and a small number are able to distinguish themselves from the majority. Although many desire to make a difference; few actually dare to do what it takes to achieve their dreams.

It is time to break the bar of mediocrity and begin thinking about living a life of impact.

Many have found out about the supernatural power from above and it has distinguished them, it has turned them from weak to strong, from fruitless to fruitful and from death to life. This supernatural power is known as THE ANOINTING of the Holy Spirit.

As a believer, heaven has invested its best in you to live a life of impact. The anointing has given you the power of God which breaks yokes and removes heavy burdens.

I hope that as you continue to read, you will discover all you need to know about the anointing because you owe it to yourself to go for the best. The greater one lives inside of you – so step into the anointing and release the power for impact!

CHAPTER 1

ANOINTED TO LEAD

God anoints all His leaders to lead. The anointing will serve as God's approval of the work He has appointed His servants. Without the anointing effectively operational in a leader's life, the leader will function in an unproductive atmosphere.

When I say leaders, I am referring to all believers from the pulpit to the pew. We are all called to lead in one capacity or another because we are all called to influence. Therefore the terms leader and believer will be used interchangeably. Wherever you find yourself as a believer you must hunger for His anointing to impact your generation.

Leaders must hunger, seek and pray for the anointing to be activated and made functional for service unto the Lord.

Isaiah 10:27 - And it shall come to pass in that day, that his burden shall be taken away from off thy shoulder, and his yoke from off thy neck, and the yoke shall be destroyed because of the anointing.

According to the above verse of scripture, the anointing is responsible for removing burdens and destroying yokes. Thus, for any significant work to be accomplished, the anointing needs to be powerfully engaged.

Being gifted with talent and charisma may carry a leader a long way, nonetheless, it is the presence of the anointing that will make the difference. It is the anointing that sets the believer apart and causes great works to be achieved. Talent and charisma cannot remove burdens or destroy yokes. This great privilege is reserved for the anointing.

In other words, the proof of God-anointed leaders will be the presence of the anointing that enables them to remove burdens and destroy yolks. It will be a sign that God is with them and that they are backed by heaven to accomplish greater works.

I pray that signs and wonders will begin to follow you in your ministry, business, city and nation.

People are suffering under heavy demonic burdens and weighed down with strong yokes. God desires to raise up spiritual leaders that can challenge the evil forces, stop their interferences and set His people free.

Are you the type of leader God can use in times like this?

Are you hungry for the power of God?

Are you lacking results?

CHAPTER 2

THE POWER OF GOD

Acts 10:38 - How God anointed Jesus of Nazareth with the Holy Ghost and with power: who went about doing good, and healing all that were oppressed of the devil; for God was with him.

Faith is not given to the believer to simply wish for better; it is given to the believer to do well. Jesus "went about doing good and healing all those who were oppressed of the devil". Jesus used the anointing, He did something with it.

The anointing is also referred to as the power of God, because wherever Jesus showed up, good things began to happen and it became evident that the power of God was working through Him. Notice that because of the anointing in the life of Jesus, His ministry produced results. *Acts 10:38* tells us how manifestations of "power" began to accompany Him.

John 3:1-2 - There was a man of the Pharisees, named Nicodemus, a ruler of the Jews: The same came to Jesus by night, and said unto him, Rabbi, <u>we know that thou art a teacher come from God: for no man can do these miracles that thou doest, except God be with him.</u>

Firstly, Jesus "went about"; in other words nothing stopped Him. He could no longer be hindered by any force whatsoever. HE was totally in control of His destiny. There was no power that could curtail His movements. Jesus became a barrier breaker. The enemy could no longer question Him or tell Him where to go or not go.

What would life be like if you were never stopped or hindered by forces that once held you back? It would be a great thing to look back at the devil with a smile and say "you were able to stop me once, but now I have defeated you!"

The anointing pushes one to function beyond their natural limitations and into areas where they begin to do the impossible. It propels the believer to exchange the usual for the unusual; the common for the uncommon and the natural for the supernatural.

I decree and declare that the devil has no power to stop you ever again and pray that the unusual, the uncommon and the supernatural will be your portion from this day onward!

Secondly, Jesus achieved good results; the scripture says He did good *(Acts 10:38)*. The anointing is the very power of God that produces good results just as God Himself would.

In the beginning whatever resulted from the produce of God, was called very GOOD *(Genesis 1:31)*. It is amazing that everything the anointing produced in the work of Christ was good.

Wouldn't you like to be producing only good to great results? That is the power of the anointing. It will force great results out of you when you are fully activated and functional under the power of God.

At times, it is very daunting when we have tried all we can yet still nothing seems to go right. More often than not, this predicament is as a result of either the enemy's burden or a yoke which is in operation. However, when the anointing comes into being it begins to do what it does best; remove burdens and destroy yokes - causing the believer to gain ground and move to higher heights.

Thirdly, the scripture declares that Jesus went about healing all those that were oppressed of the devil. At the time, this was peculiar and unheard of. It was surprising to His generation that a man could command such authority and power. They were dumbfounded, as in His presence all the forces of the devil melted off the lives of people that were once held bound. Oppression also disappeared right in the face of the anointing, and no trace of oppression was found after Jesus dealt with the powers that be.

I see God using you to do the same and even more!

Sicknesses and diseases are not mere natural occurrences, Jesus identified the devil as the 'brains' behind sickness and disease *(Matthew 8:16, Matthew 12:22 and John 10:10)*. Both sickness and disease are under the curse and Christ, The Anointed One and His Anointing, has redeemed us from the curse *(Galatians 3:13-14)*. You can chase away diseases and you can dismantle the power of the oppressor because of the anointing.

I pray that you will no longer be oppressed by the devil from today in Jesus name.

Pray today, under the authority of Jesus, and command every oppressive force to melt away and disappear.

Fourthly, the scripture says "God was with Him". The anointing is the very presence of God. The anointing is the seal of approval that God has come with you to accomplish all that He has asked you to do.

The old hymn "Blessed Assurance Jesus is mine," brings to light the very essence of God being with the believer. This 'assurance' is knowing that through the anointing the believer draws comfort that God is present and is working with them. Assurance breeds confidence; knowing that wherever you go, God stands with you to accomplish greater works.

The word says, "If God be for you who can be against you?" *(Romans 8:31)*

Through the Bible we read that during His time on earth, Jesus demonstrated and walked in blessed assurance and this assurance produced levels of great boldness in His ministry.

In the face of daily threats on His life, Jesus worked none stop and gained ground doing mighty miracles as He moved closer toward His goal; all because the Father was with Him. Jesus walked with power and boldness because the Father had charged and empowered Him with the anointing. He walked amongst the people and those against Him could not touch Him, arrest Him or kill Him - because God was with Him. In the end He would lay His life down on His own accord, yet promised to take it back. That is power!

John 10:17 - Therefore doth my Father love me, because I lay down my life, that I might take it again.

Prayer points

1. Nothing can touch my destiny because I am anointed in Jesus name
2. Refuse the temptation to judged your life based on your abilities or qualities
3. Provoke all God's abilities to manifest in your life

CHAPTER 3

ENGAGING THE ANOINTING

Luke 24:49 - And, behold, I send the promise of my Father upon you: but tarry ye in the city of Jerusalem, until ye be endued with power from on high.

The anointing ensures a life of signs and wonders. If there are no signs in your life to prove that you are working for God whether in ministry, business, home life, work or anything that you claim God has entrusted in your hands, then it is time to hunger for the anointing.

There is no more time for trial and error. God is looking for a man or woman who is ready to provoke His anointing to unthinkable limits. YES! He can entrust you with His burden removing, yoke destroying power from above. After all, He told the Apostles to wait for it, and when it came the Apostles impacted and transformed their world.

Acts 17:6 - and when they found them not, they drew Jason and certain brethren unto the rulers of the city, crying, These that have turned the world upside down are come hither also;

Before this time all the apostles had were memories of the powerful acts of Christ. I am sure they began telling stories of the five thousand who were fed with fishes and loaves. They must have remembered when Jesus walked on water. Peter must have shook his head in agreement of the awe they must have felt and John would have been able to describe the heartbeat of Jesus. Even with all these amazing memories, God had more for them. The events that took place with Jesus were not the end to the purpose of their calling.

When the anointing came and they engaged, it automatically turned them from history tellers to history makers. They were turned from fearful men to faithful men, from powerless men to powerful men.

By partnering with the anointing they were upgraded to the miracle working life. They got results and they became outstanding people of their times. They were transformed from the state of depression to oppressors of the devil everywhere they went. The gates of hell could no longer hold people bound because these men waited on and engaged with the anointing.

Daniel 11:32 - And such as do wickedly against the covenant shall he corrupt by flatteries: but the people that do know their God shall be strong, and do exploits.

I see you making history!

I see you turning your world upside down to the glory of God!

Engaging the anointing will bring the believer to the realm of action, it will transport the believer to the manifested power of God with signs following. It is imperative to say this: do not leave everything to chance. If something in your life is not working - engage the anointing.

God has called you for results and not religion! His anointing in your life is a sure sign that you are called into active duty. The anointing in you is that stamp of approval that qualifies you to lead the supernatural life. So become active and results will begin to manifest all around you.

The activation of the anointing that is reserved in you is a scary thought to the enemy. He does not want you to realise the power in the anointing and so he comes up with great schemes, religious activities and programs to distract you from seeking the authentic power of God. He will not give you rest on every side, he causes things to go wrong, feel wrong and look wrong; but when you engage with the anointing, all the enemy's schemes and tricks will melt away.

2 Chronicles 16:9a - For the eyes of the LORD run to and fro throughout the whole earth, to shew himself strong in the behalf of them whose heart is perfect toward him...

Engaging the anointing attracts the attention of heaven. Heaven is drawn to a believer who hungers enough to be used by God. Heaven will spring into supernatural action for anyone whose will is to do what it takes to walk in the anointing of God. The eyes of the Lord are looking for you because He wants to show Himself strong on your behalf.

I pray that as you engage the anointing today, heaven will open up and you will experience days of heaven on earth!

CHAPTER 4

UNDERSTANDING THE ANOINTING

Luke 4:17-19 - And there was delivered unto him the book of the prophet Esaias. And when he had opened the book, he found the place where it was written, 18 The Spirit of the Lord is upon me, because he hath anointed me to preach the gospel to the poor; he hath sent me to heal the broken-hearted, to preach deliverance to the captives, and recovering of sight to the blind, to set at liberty them that are bruised, 19 To preach the acceptable year of the Lord.

Jesus found Himself in the book of Isaiah. As He read the passage and believed the word of God, He located His anointing. We read that Jesus submitted to the fact that it is the anointing that empowered Him to preach the gospel to the poor. Notice that even poverty is a burden and yoke that needs the anointing to remove and destroy it.

Poverty is a demonically orchestrated act as we can see across the globe. The enemy fights to spread the spirit of poverty through wars, greed and climatological conditions. Our confidence can rest in the fact that the Lord has already empowered the Church and individual believers with tremendous power that can bring about positive change into situations no matter how terrible and atrocious they are.

The anointing is a more potent and powerful force that will destroy any yoke and remove any burden, even that of poverty.

Again, it is the anointing that empowered Jesus to heal the broken hearted. Where mere words could not reach or touch, the anointing was able to bring about total restoration to the broken hearted.

Cold heartedness is an evil that has plagued this generation. Due to this evil, many have suffered harsh rejection of various kinds. The predicaments of joblessness, the pain of homelessness, the tragedies of divorce, teen challenges, the unfortunate situation of teen pregnancies, suicidal tendencies and loneliness are just some of the burdens and yokes the enemy is using. In doing so, the enemy has turned many to addictive living simply to numb the effect of pain and sorrow; locked up behind unseen prison bars it seems as though there is no hope.

Thanks be to God for the anointing! Through the anointing the believer can operate in the same dimensions as Jesus and bring about restoration, wellbeing and great healing to our communities. These desired transformations can only manifest by the power of God. How hungry are you? Can you be used by God for transformation? Do not step back and wait for a special person – you are that special person!

Furthermore *Luke 4:17-19* declares that the blind can receive their sight. Many who were once physically blind received their sight because of the anointing.

What about spiritually blinded individuals? These are cases where people are in a state of confusion, full of doubt concerning their future and trapped in a vicious circle of wrong choices because of blindness. People who are under such heavy burdens usually suffer from some kind of identity crises because their mind has lost the essence of who they really.

The anointing will effectively break such yokes, open spiritual eyes and impact the mind so much so that there will be a burst of fresh ideas and concepts. The anointing works strongly to restore the mind and empowers creativity, so that the individual will respond to who they really are.

Pray: *I command every yoke of confusion brakes away in Jesus name*

Lastly the scripture in Luke highlights that the anointing of Jesus was evidenced in the power of setting at liberty those that are bruised in life. It declares that they can be set free. To be bruised is to be shattered or smitten through and through and broken by life's troubles. There is no limit as to how the anointing can work. Even the shattered can miraculously be gathered and put back together as brand new.

After the great flood, Noah had to wait for the water to subside. While he was waiting the scripture records that God remembered Noah. Metaphorically the word 'remember', depicts Noah being torn apart by preceding events. Thousands were destroyed in the floods and one can only imagine the anguish in Noah's heart and the emptiness and fear he may have experienced, but the Bible says God remembered Noah. God came to Noah's rescue and literally pieced him back together again. God lined up his soul back to a place of tranquillity by cutting a new covenant of peace with him.

Similarly the anointing of God can bring anything to life, no matter how shattered it may be. Gods anointing has the ability to piece lives back together miraculously. Anointed leaders must be powerful and effective in these last days, they must stand out with major demonstrations of signs and wonders to restore the bruised. God's plan and desire is that more leaders, who are hungry to possess the great and mighty power of God, will rise up.

As leaders all believers need to hunger for higher levels of the demonstration and manifestation of the anointing that will distinguish them and their work for God. The anointing can set every believer apart in a world that is so used to impressive images. From silver screen to the big screen - you need the anointing to demonstrate the glory of God and cause an impact that cannot be erased.

CHAPTER 5

DEFINING THE ANOINTING

Every key leader in the Bible functioned under the anointing and the blessing of God.

In the Old Testament we read that when God blessed an individual it revealed that God was with that individual. Joseph is an excellent example, the scriptures say in *Genesis 39:29* "And the LORD was with Joseph, and he was a prosperous man; and he was in the house of his master the Egyptian."

God was with Joseph and due to his association with God, Joseph prospered. Joseph walked in manifested results. In the same vein the New Testament reiterates that when God anoints an individual it is equal to His being present with that individual for an impactful life. So whenever you come across the word 'blessed' or 'anointing', they may read different but both carry the presence and the approval of God.

Definition of the Anointing

The word anointing literally means to smear on, to rub on or to consecrate in. This means that every know leader that impacted their generation in the scriptures, had something special smeared on them that distinguished them from the rest. God rubbed on them the anointing that made them shine differently to their peers.

Their peculiar hunger to be servants to the things of God, attracted the presence of God so much so that they left indelible marks of impact.

The anointing consecrated them and set them apart from the rest. God wants to set you apart and make you different from the world so you can impact your generation, with your gifting and talents for the glory of God.

Fourteen people are specially noted in scripture as being anointed for a unique task or responsibility. They are Aaron and his four sons to serve as priests *(Exodus 29:7-9)*, Saul *(1 Samuel 10:1)*, David *(1 Samuel 16:13)* and Solomon *(1 Kings 1:39)* who all served as kings over Israel. David's son Absalom, who tried to take the throne of his father but was killed in the process *(2 Samuel 19:10)*, was also anointed by someone to be king. Whilst this was a case self-appointment, Absalom's interim kingship was endorsed by the anointing which was conferred upon him by the people and it was significant enough to force the rightful King, David, into exile. King Jehu of Israel *(2 Kings 9:6)*, Elisha - prophet in Elijah's stead *(1 King 19:16)* and Kings Joash *(2 Kings 11:12)* and Jehoahaz *(2 Kings 23:30)* of Judah were also anointed. JESUS of Nazareth was ANOINTED King over all. *(Luke 4:18)*

CHAPTER 6

STIRRING UP THE ANOINTING

The word of God boldly declares that the believer has been anointed.

1 John 2:27 - But the anointing which ye have received of him abideth in you, and ye need not that any man teach you: but as the same anointing teacheth you of all things, and is truth, and is no lie, and even as it hath taught you, ye shall abide in him

Many do not believe that they have been anointed and so they do not know how to provoke the anointing into manifestation. They are walking with the power of God on the inside yet still operate with their natural human power. *(Philippians 4:13)*

A vast amount of believers have no clear understanding of how powerful they are on the inside because they have believed the enemy's lie of how weak they are on the outside. They have accepted that the power of God is for a chosen few when God already deposited all His power inside of them. *(Matthew 28:18-19 and 1 John 4:4)*

Failing to realise that the resurrection power of God dwells within, many believers have given up on their desire and hunger to excel in life and to experience the power of God. *(Romans 8:11)*

All believers have received the burden removing, yoke destroying power from heaven. So why does it look like only some have received the anointing and not all? Why is it that the enemy looks like he has the advantage over many believers? The answer is because very few provoke the anointing to work in their lives. Yes! The anointing needs to be provoked! "How?" you may say.

Notice the anointing is depicted as the power of God, however in the natural it is compared to oil. As God instructed Moses to prepare the anointing oil; we also need to prepare fully to provoke the anointing.

Exodus 30:25 - And thou shalt make it an oil of holy ointment, an ointment compound after the art of the apothecary: it shall be an holy anointing oil.

Exodus 30:31 - And thou shalt speak unto the children of Israel, saying, This shall be an holy anointing oil unto me throughout your generations.

In other words, the anointing is depicted as oil or can be compared to behave as oil would.

Firstly it is liquid and is only required to be applied when needed. Many do not even bother to consciously activate their senses daily to remember that the power from on high dwells in them. They walk out and that is it; they never declare how anointed they are. Most people will only declare when they are already deep in trouble, they say things like "but wait I am anointed, why so much trouble?" Although their concerns are voiced late, the anointing will always help them - but that is not the point. The key is remembering and declaring on a daily basis that you are anointed.

Pray: *I activate the anointing today in Jesus name*

In other words, just like the palm of your hands activate and spread all the fragrance in your body lotion, likewise, your tongue will activate all the properties of the anointing to come alive around your affairs.

Activate the power of the anointing through your proclamation and affirmation. Do you know that you can even direct the anointing to a place of pressing need even before you get there? You can say "the anointing has gone before me and it is working for me right now in my interview, job, negotiation, building project, doctors report," and so forth.

Secondly, if the jar of oil is not used frequently all the properties might settle at the bottom of the jar. Likewise, the anointing can become dormant and all the powers made redundant in the lives of individuals who are not willing to take godly counselling and guidance, nor are they willing for God to shake them out there comfort zones. You need a shaking to activate the anointing.

It is a sad picture of many who assume that in doing nothing the anointing will provoke God to action and rescue them. No matter the power and forces of righteousness that reside in you as a believer; they only flow through the anointing that must first be stirred up.

Thirdly, when the temperature in a room drops oil can become congealed and cannot move around anymore. This is a terrible state and we see it frequently where believers can hardly pray the way they should. The Lord Jesus put it this way – "And because iniquity shall abound, the love of many shall wax cold" (Matthew

24:12). This is the state and condition where individuals no longer believe and trust in godly processes and principles; where they settle for mechanical religion and goodwill, having the form of godliness but denying the power of God.

Prayer points

1.   Lord set me on fire
2.   Make me a testimony

CHAPTER 7

PROVOKING THE ANOINTING

Hebrews 1:9 - Thou hast loved righteousness, and hated iniquity; therefore God, even thy God, hath anointed thee with the oil of gladness above thy fellows.

Firstly, love righteousness

The anointing will only be allowed to flow in the life of the individual who falls in love with the word of God. You cannot spend time in the living word and remain dead. The recipient of the word of life will definitely become a distributor of power and life because the word of God is alive and powerful.

Mark 12:24 - And Jesus answering said unto them, Do ye not therefore err, because ye know not the scriptures, neither the power of God?

To provoke the anointing one needs to imbibe the words of righteousness; one needs to fall in love with the truth. Falling in love with the word is falling love with Jesus The Anointed One and His Anointing. *(John 1:1, 14 and 1 Corinthians 1:30)*

The word of God is anointed enough to provoke the reservoirs of life in you to move into action. Get the word in you and your life shall move to unimaginable heights.

Loving righteousness is a powerful key to releasing the anointing because the anointing is a righteous force and only lovers of righteousness can provoke its wonder working properties. *(John 1:4)*

Secondly, hate iniquity

Here is another valuable key that will provoke the anointing in you: hating sin.

Detesting sin is a major way to provoke the anointing in your life. These days it may seem unnecessary to deal with sin, but the truth of the matter is that in order to command uncommon signs and wonders you need to hate sin. Unrighteousness and iniquitous tendencies are serious hindrances when you desire to provoke the anointing.

The anointing is Gods approval on the work of His servant. The anointing is the very presence of God; it simply shows that God is present with an individual. So if an individual allows sin to be present, then God will be absent. The scripture says:

1 John 1:5 - This then is the message which we have heard of him, and declare unto you, that God is light, and in him is no darkness at all.

If God is light and there is no darkness in Him then surely if the individual remains in darkness, the power of light and the forces of light will become ineffective in their lives; hence the anointing will never work. Jesus delivered us from darkness so that the anointing can be released without measure. *(Colossians 1:13)*

Thirdly, become a lover of the souls of men

Jesus' first declaration as to the purpose of His anointing is to preach to the poor; He desired for people to be saved. *(Luke 19:10)*

The anointing is in you for somebody else to be saved from sin, death, disease and poverty - to mention a few. The anointing can only be released when we have others in mind. You have been empowered for somebody else and your reservoir of power is to satisfy or bring life to another person.

Have you noticed that containers never enjoy what they carry for themselves? Their joy however is to see the smile on the faces of their users who enjoy what they have carried.

The ultimate joy of the anointed leader is to experience the power of God at work in the lives of people they touch with the anointing. This key will ignite more power in your spirit because it is the heart of God that we love others and preach the gospel. As you purpose to love souls, it may become difficult because you will have to love at all times - but keep on track, keep on loving and provoking the anointing!

I declare you shall be celebrated!

I declare your life shall be different and be used for signs and wonders.

I declare that you will not be deprived from enjoying the power of the anointing reserved in you.

I pray that you see more reasons to be a blessing to others.

I also pray that as you provoke the anointing, fresh ideas and concepts will be deposited into your heart and mind.

I pray that your focus will remain on the revelation that others need help from God.

Fourthly, live a prayerful life. (Matthew 17:21)

In the scriptures everyone that succeeded in God, did so with prayer. There is something that happens to the person who chooses to set proper time apart in prayer. Prayer shows a humble heart. Prayer shows that one relies heavily on God. Prayer shows that one hungers to have fellowship with God. Prayers shows that the believer loves the presence of God.

When I refer to the realms of prayer, I am also referring to praying in the spirit or speaking in the language of the Holy Spirit. This power practice will enable the believers' spirit to become even more built up. The believer will be able to lift up and carry heavy revelations that can alter physical conditions. Praying in the spirit allows for God to expose spiritual truths. This truly fires up the anointing reservoir for great impact. (Jude 1:20)

Fifth, live a fasted life.

This is a sure way of provoking levels of anointing that will gush out of the spirit with endless supernatural powers. Fasting releases tremendous power that will astound even the believer at times. Fasting acts like a power cleansing solution that cleanses the spiritual pipeline from dross. Fasting will radically cleanse the believer teaching them how to flow in the forces of righteousness for a life of impact.

Fasting will revitalise your spiritual senses as it acts as a cleanser to all your spiritual receptors. This will cause the believer to possess heightened sensitivity to the anointing of God. The believer will be super charged after a period of fasting. Just like the following men in the Bible after their times of fasting:

- *Jesus fasted 40 days (Luke 4:2)*
- *Moses fasted 40 days (Exodus 34:28)*
- *Nehemiah fasted (Nehemiah 1:4)*
- *The Israelites fasted in the days of Queen Esther (Esther 9:31)*
- *David fasted (Psalm 109:24)*
- *Daniel fasted (Daniel 9:3)*
- *Jeremiah fasted (Jeremiah 36:6)*
- *Anna fasted (Luke 2:37)*
- *The Apostles would fast (Matthew 9:15)*
- *Cornelius fasted (Acts 10:30)*

After fasting these individuals mightily impacted their generations with the mind of God. Their lives made a difference and people were blessed because of their sacrifices. Our generation has a need for the intervention of the power of God like never before: It is time to make an impact! The enemy has been on the rampage for too long in our communities and needs to be stopped with the power of God.

This is the good news – God has already placed the necessary power within every believer!

Sixth, fall in love with the worship of God through songs, hymns and spiritual songs

When the temple of Solomon was completed God released His glory in the atmosphere and the priests could no longer stand on their feet. Everybody fell to the ground in awe of the presence of God. *(1 Kings 8:10-11)*

The word of God refers to the believer as the temple of the living God. (2 Corinthians 6:16). When the believer falls in love with worshiping God the power of God and the anointing ebbs to heights that are unprecedented and will distinguish the believer.

Seventh, live a life of faith.

The scripture declares that faith pleases God. Intoxicated by faith, the men of old obeyed God and moved greatly to accomplish major things for Him. The anointing always flourishes in the realm of faith *(Hebrews 11:6)*

It is by faith that one can truly understand and use the anointing and the power that flows from God. Faith challenges the realm of logic and dismantles its energy because logic often tries to hinder the force of faith.

Also, through faith we are able break the sound barrier of fear, which tries to speak loud volumes of unbelief. The believer that will engage with the anointing must stay in the realm of faith long enough for the anointing to begin its powerful work. The anointing then becomes that dynamic force that empowers faith to do what faith does best; overcome the impossible and achieve the miraculous.

You are anointed for great exploits. God has called you and anointed you personally to achieve great things, so make it happen!

And it shall come to pass in that day, that his burden shall be taken away from off thy shoulder, and his yoke from off thy neck, and the yoke shall be destroyed because of the anointing.

Isaiah 10:27

9 789082 411706